Pages

When the pages of my life
come to an end I want you to know
that you were the most beautiful chapter
and if I were to read it again
I would start at the chapter we first met.

Reviews

"Bonita's writing is wonderful, generous, brave – and rings true with the sincerity and integrity of an ancient singing bowl gong. Thank you for sharing it with me."
A.M.

"Bonita's poetry is nourishing, there is something for everyone. A copy should be on the shelf of each persons home."
Cynthia L.J.

"A wonderful read. Bonita's poetry is soulful, moving and inspiring, her poems can relate to many people going through different situations in life."
Grazia Noveri

Acknowledgements

To my family and friends who have always believed in me and inspired me to write. Thank you for your continued love, support, and encouragement. Without you this book would still be pages in my mind locked away from the world to read.

I would like to thank all the woman from my WOW (Woman Only Writing) group for their endless support, laughter and shared enthusiasm and passion for writing. And Shirley G, author and tutor, for facilitating our group and continued motivation, writing prompts, shared writing material and constructive critique.

To my loving partner George who read and re-read my poetry with excitement and awe. Your contribution, creative design and layout of my book is phenomenal.

This book is dedicated to my two beautiful children, April and Keanin.

You are the light that never dims
You are the love that never fails
You are the laughter that never dies
you are...
My happiness and everything in between.

I am a *Mother*,
a *Lover*,
and a *Poet*.

I don't subscribe to labels.
Passion is my drive,
love is my force
and *family is everything*.

A collection of 122 poems,
You & I = Us,
is a collection of poetry from my first edition:
April Moon – Poetry for the Soul (2018) and my enhanced edition(2019).

Poetry for me is an expression of art through words, my collection of poems are soulful, nourishing, moving and brave.

I have shared some of my most intimate and personal experiences in this book and hope to evoke feelings that are real and raw in anyone who reads it.

This is my journey, my testament.

Contents

Lost	1
Wicklow waves	2
Voice	3
Acceptance	4
Apology	5
Another empty bottle	6
Fearless love	7
If I wrote a book for you	8
Don't settle for less	9
Thoughts from my window pane	10
Falling for you	11
Forever kind of love	12
Fragments of me	14
Frail	15
Grieving the loss of you	16
Time is of the essence	17
Bullying is not okay	18
Pages of a broken love story	20
I lost my heart	21
I miss you	22
I once was	23
I surrender myself	24
I wept	25
I will wait for you	26
Against all my fears	27
Things I would tell you	28
A love between Mother and Child	29
Surreal	30

Believe	31
Beautiful life	33
Kissing	34
Broken	35
Love letter	36
Loveless games	40
More	41
Heart beat	42
But for love	43
Never changing	44
Once in a lifetime	45
Brave	47
Desert of my dreams	48
Heartache	49
My life	50
A world forever changing	52
My demise	53
Seekers	54
Weekend lover	55
Again	56
This is me	57
Life	58
What if	59
Original	60
Liquid	61
Playlist	62
Music	63
Find your way back	64

No quick fix	65
Another life	66
Undone	67
Love that came without warning	68
But you left me anyway	69
You don't see me	71
Invisible strings	72
Love	73
Stepping stones	74
I am You are	76
Expression	77
Counter tops	78
Forgiveness	79
Fleeting moment	80
What is love?	81
You are worthy	82
Your spell	84
Surrendered kiss	85
When is it my turn	86
The forest	87
Two hearts	88
My favourite painting	89
Ultimate sacrifice	90
Lovers	91
A promise	92
Un-kissed	94
Poetry and dreams	95
Love child	96

The spaces between us	99
Letting go	100
Dance with me	101
Thank you	102
Reminiscing	104
Life happens	105
Conversations	106
Destiny	107
...In love...	108
Stolen	109
* I will I am	110
Name	111
* Blind love	112
Getting to know me	113
* Something like a phenomenon	114
* Picture this	115
Let's walk the earth together	116
Tides	117
Speak to me	118
* A kiss so fair	119
* Thinking of you	120
Love juice	121
* Let's have fun tonight	122
The bridge of...	124
* Thoughts and shared words	125
* Tantric bliss	126
Song	127
* Adventure	128

Dance floor	129
* *I see you*	130
Verbal abuse	131
Shadows and gold	132
* *Tender words*	133
Lucky Love	134
Waking dream	135
Car crash	136
Me	137
Log out...	138

* *Co-written by Bonita Moscos and George Xafis*

Lost

Empty emotions I carry deep within
my thoughts haunt me I cannot win
I fear I have lost myself.

I long to find some inner peace
I long to find what's lost in me
my weary heart has travelled far.

Where do I begin?

Wicklow waves

Wicklow waves crashing on the pebble beach
sand and stone beneath my feet.

The wind whispering secret thoughts out loud.

As I gaze up
sun and clouds
I say your name ....

Voice

My heart is in my voice
and that is why I write poetry.

Acceptance

I think sometimes people are afraid
to accept the person you are
because that would mean
they would have to accept themselves...

Apology

There comes a time when there are only
so many apologies one can make
to mend a broken mind
heart or soul.

There is only so much you can say
till the words pour dry form your mouth.

There is only so much pain
and guilt you can feel
till you become numb
and you can feel no more.

There is only so much ink you can spill
for all the letters
poems and words you write till your pen runs dry.

There comes a point when you have said
and done all you can
and you have felt broken
and tired in your bones.

And if all you have said and done
is not enough
it never will be.
So I've let it go and know now
that this too shall pass...

Another empty bottle

As I stare down another empty bottle
and reminisce my time with you
I am reminded of how you saw me
this wild young girl who had seen so much hurt
felt so much pain
grew up way before her time
But you took me as I was
you helped me heal
you helped me live you made me love.

You stole my heart
you saw past all my madness
and I made you mine.

Together we created life
a boy so extraordinary
who we would love so fiercely
a bond forever unbroken no matter what life threw at us.

We shared love
we shared laughter
we shared tears and anger
joy and pain
but through all the years we remained constant
through all the chaos
the distance the challenges
We were and would always be foremost parents.
I will forever keep you in my heart.

Fearless love

It is what I call a fearless love

A love with no boundaries and no expectations
a pure and selfless love.
A love with no questions only trust
communication
hope and adoration

For one another.

Filled with endless hugs
kisses
and sometimes tears...
But in the end
there is no fear.

If I wrote a book for you

If I wrote a book for you would you read to the end?
If I sang a song for you would you listen?
If I gave you all of me would you be content?
As the rivers flow into the ocean, deserts dry in the sand
storms break
trees and flowers bloom and yet the leaves fall.

Will you still love me through it all?

After time everything fades but my love for you will still remain
And as time moves on and seasons change
through the joy and laughter we share
through the hurt and the tears
there is you the smile on my lips
the soft whisper in my ear
you who quietens my fear.

You the gentle touch on my skin
and the love from within
T h e r e   i s   y o u .

Don't settle for less

Life is full of mystery's waiting to be discovered...

We all search for a belonging
a wanting of something more
something pure.

Yet we forget to discover
that within ourselves...
What we are capable of
who we are
and what makes us unique...

Don't forget your roots
what you are worth.
And don't settle for less
than what you deserve.

Thoughts from my window pane

As I sit here watching the sunset from my window pane
I wonder where you are

I wonder how far I would go to feel your warm embrace
your cheek pressed next to mine
the warmth of your breath against my neck
and the sweet kiss that lingers on my lips.

Your hands pulling me close as you hold me so tightly;
I can feel your heartbeat against my skin...

...So tonight I will dream
I will let it go
I will let it be
I will fall into you
and you into me.

Falling for you

I am weak, and I am falling
like the stars that fall from the sky
the moon from the sun
the tides from the ocean.

I am captivated by your soul.

You have broken me wide open
and I am drowning in your love.

With just one look
and the smile on your lips
I know that I am forever yours.

Forever kind of love

I believe in a forever kind of love
A *love* that lifts you up when you feel at your lowest
A *love* that makes you smile at the sound of their voice
A *love* that makes your heart beat faster at the sight
of their number or message showing up on your phone
A *love* that makes you question why you ever thought
you were not good enough for someone else
A *love* that makes you realize that being crazy in love is okay
That too much of a good love is not a bad thing
A *love* that sees your imperfections and loves you anyway
A *love* that opens your mind
A *love* that loves you without judgment
A *love* that challenges you
A *love* that supports and encourages your future goals
A *love* that makes you believe in yourself
A *love* that stays even during difficult times
A *love* that fights through the bad times
to get through to the good times
A *love* that won't abandon you
The kind of *love* where you go to bed cuddling
and kissing even after a fight
A *love* that is carefree and fun and exciting
but can sometimes be routine and boring and that's okay
A *love* where communication is key
and trust, loyalty and honesty is put above all else
A *love* where you can have fun with each other
and filled with laughter and silliness
A *love* who offers a shoulder to cry on when you're feeling down

A *love* that understands talking about problems is part
of being together
A *love* that is understanding
A *love* where you can scream and shout when things
don't always go the way you planned
because realistically nothing is set in stone
A *love* where you can be yourself
sometimes loud and sometimes quiet
A *love* where you can share early morning walks
to watch the sunrise or chase the moon and stars at midnight
A *love* that has no boundaries
A *love* that is pure and deep and honest
A *love* that is filled with passion
A *love* where at the age of 90 you still hold hands
walking down the street
or sitting beside each other
A *love* when you truly see the beauty in each other
after years of being together
A *love* that puts family above everything else
A *love* worth making sacrifices for
A *love* you can trust
A *love* you can share your deepest darkest secrets with
A *love* you can share your fears with
and they won't use it against you
A *love* that grows stronger and deeper as the years go by
A *love* that brings out the best in you
A *love* that chooses you
      A *forever love,* my *forever kind* of love

Fragments of me

These are the fragments of me I allow you to see
Fragments of myself
hidden behind my eyes
my smile
my mind...

These fragments will take a lifetime to explore
and forevermore to adore.

If only you stay just for a while
and seek what's hidden behind this face
these eyes
this smile
maybe you will get more
than just fragments

Maybe you will get all of me.

Frail

Even as you held me
and kissed my tears away
you walked out the door
leaving me so frail.

Even as I closed my eyes
and wished for you to stay
I held onto the hope
that you'd return to me some day.

Even as the hours turned into days
and nights
I dreamt of you coming home
and holding onto me
so tight.

Even when my soul is aching
I still cannot hate you for leaving
while my heart was breaking.

Even if I never see you again
I know I will love you
and I was loved in return.

Grieving the loss of you

I cannot control my tears
They come in waves and knock me off my feet
when I least expect it.

I close my eyes and wonder about your thoughts
in those last moments
I think about the darkness
and loneliness you must have experienced

I wish I had the chance to say goodbye

You weren't supposed to leave...

You were supposed to grow old
watch your children finish school
start careers
get married
start a family
and become a grandparent.

You weren't supposed to leave...
You were supposed to live...

Time is of the essence

Here is what only time will tell.

Time is limited
time has a beginning and an end
time waits for no one.

Yet time is measured by foolish people
with foolish expectations
that consumes and rules them
only because they have been conformed to believe so.

Time is of the essence they say
but essence is character
spirit
soul
nature and life...

Time is what we make of it.

How we embrace it
and choose to live through it
Well that is entirely
a different aspect
of time.

Bullying is not okay

I am not the girl you see in the halls smiling
while inside my heart is crying.

I am not the girl with the perfect skin
and beautiful hair
with bright blue eyes
and not a care...

I am the girl you taunt at day
while you laugh and curse
and look my way.

I am girl that tries to hide the pain
I carry deep inside

Your words
your hate
consumes my mind

I carry this burden;
there is no escape in my realm of time...

Until one day I reached out

I searched my soul
there you were a glimmer of hope
a shimmer of light
you gave me strength to not give up

but the *will* to fight
Your words can no longer break me

Your hate will no longer consume me

Your laughter will no longer taunt me.

Here I stand strong and tall
this girl you hurt
I am no more...

Pages of a broken love story

I am pages of broken love stories
one with endless beginnings and endings...
When all I want is to be someone's love story
one you can read from beginning to end.

I lost my heart

I watch the heavens while I am walking down the street

I soak up the brilliant light of the morning;

I look up at the sun and think of you

and wonder where did it all go so wrong?

Was I so blind not to see the signs which lay before me?

Everything changes and falls apart

I cannot stand to lose myself

you left

and I lost my heart.

I miss you

I miss you like the ocean misses the sand

I miss you like sky misses the sun

I miss you like the moon misses the stars

I miss you like the earth misses the water

I miss you like rivers flow to the sea

I miss you like wild fires that spread through the forests

I miss you as the birds need their morning song

I miss you in the day as I would in the night

I miss the taste of your mouth pressed against mine

I miss the warmth of your breathe against my cheek

I miss your eyes lighting up when you see my morning smile

I miss your sweet embrace when you held me tight

I miss you more with each passing day.

I once was

I once was the smiling face who greeted you at the front door
I once was the lips you kissed and arms you embraced
but I am no more.

I once was the one you called to tell me about your day
the voice I loved to hear and things to me you'd say.

I once was the woman you could never live without.
I once was the woman in whom you never had a doubt.
I once was the woman you loved and needed most.
I once was the woman with whom you shared your dreams
and hopes.

I once was the woman you slept with at night
tangled up in our embrace as we held each other tight.

We once were everything we loved and needed from each other.
But now we are just memories of what we once were...

I surrender myself

My pulse quickens
my heart beats louder with each note you sing
my breath escapes me with the beauty of your voice.

With my eyes closed and the smile on my lips
I surrender myself to the music;

I surrender myself to your song.

I wept

On this floor I wept
I wept for every broken heart
Every broken soul
And every broken mind
But mostly I wept for mine...

I will wait for you

I will wait for you in the summer breeze
I will wait for you in the winter snow
I will wait for you in the spring
till the trees blossom and leaves grow
I will wait for you in the autumn glow
and when the leaves and flowers fall

I will wait for you through it all

I will wait.

Against all my fears

Against all my fears and instincts I long for you
the deepest
darkest
rawest part of you
I long to be with you
secretive
curious
beautiful you.
I long to see you
pure
scared
wanting
forever changing you.

Searching you

Only you...

Unquestionably you
Undoubtedly you.

So I will wait
and know that someday you will find me.

Things I would tell you

In my head I tell you all the things I cannot say...
How the sun shines brighter when I wake up with you next to me.
How when you smile and kiss me I fall into a million pieces
How your eyes light up the room and time stands still.

How I still think it's a beautiful dream from which I will wake up.
How being wrapped in your arms is the best feeling in the world.
How a message from you puts a smile on my face
And the way you look at me makes my heart skip a beat
and makes my insides flutter like a butterfly.

A love between Mother and Child

In the most profound moment of sadness you are my joy
my light
my love
my laughter
my heart beat.

You share with me your secrets
you know no pain only kindness.
You see no bad only good
your innocence so pure
and your love so real;
with you I have no fear.

Thank you for choosing me to be your Mother

Your friend
your protector in this world of uncertainty.
My children you will forever be.

Surreal

In the waking of my dreams

it is your eyes I see looking back at me...

In the echo of my thoughts

it is your voice that whispers in my ear...

In the blindness of my tears

it is you who takes away my fears...

In the darkest of the night

it is your touch that fills my heart with love.

Believe

In this world we suffer in love and pain
we feel hurt
tragedy
joy
happiness
sadness
fear

But gain strength.

Strength in moving on
through our anger
our sadness our loss
our pain
through Love and learning to let go...

Let go of the past
and embrace the future
hold onto hope
hope of peace
of acceptance
of joy and of love
and of knowing that we cannot change what was meant to be
and what we have been living for.

Believe

Believe in happiness

magic
fairy tales
and have faith
faith in what the future will bring and in God
the Universe
and in life
this life and the life thereafter.

So don't let go
hold onto that love
that magic
that fairy tale
that dream.

Believe in the good and it will be yours
at the right time
and the right moment
all will be as it's meant to be.
Here in this moment
this life
in the now.

Beautiful life

Life is beautiful with you

I am learning to love you everyday

I can't live my life without you

Your smile is what keeps me going during the day

You have awakened something inside me

I thought was gone forever

You deserve everything

You are a diamond and diamonds are not easy to find

Life is better when you are loved by the person

you share your life with

When I am with you

the whole world stands still;

it is just *you*

and *me.*

Kissing

Kissing...
That sensational feeling of our mouths touching
sparks and saliva flowing
our lips pressed against each other
the warmth of our breaths that escape into one another
as we gasp for air while kissing for fear of breaking the spell.

Tongue on tongue
        cheek in cheek
tasting
        licking
playing
        biting
nibbling
        and teasing.

The beginning of promises
of passion,
        of wanting
of needing
        a sense of hunger
a connection
        of acceptance
of lust
        of love

A promise...
        And for a few, a promise of us.

Broken

It took one kiss
              for my heart to lose its balance
as I stood before you fragile
                    and b r o k e n
Yet you held me so close
        I could feel your heart beat against my chest.
You spoke to me in silence
                    your words filled the room
I am naked to your touch
                    I surrender myself to you.
      Even in my darkest hour you loved me
to the point of no return
and in that moment I came to realise that love too

                            is sometimes b r o k e n.

Love letter

If I had the courage to tell you how I felt
I would tell you that being with you scares me
and comforts me at the same time
that I get butterflies when I see you
no matter what time of day
and when you call me I get lost in your voice.

That you make me feel safe and happy
and when your arms are wrapped around me
I feel warm and fuzzy inside
and I know I am at home.

When you kiss me it's like my mouth has known no other
when we kiss, you kiss me silent
and my heart beats only for you.
When you look at me I fall into a million pieces
and I know that I am loved.

When we are together I lose all inhibition
all reason and time stands still.
It's just you and me in this uncertain world.
You make me question everything
I thought I knew I wanted
with you I feel complete, I feel at one
with you I want to explore life as
it happens the good and bad.

With you I want to build a future
a foundation

a home.
I would tell you that my soul knew you
before I knew you...
That my heart found you long before I did.

That you excite me to my core
and when we are passionate my heart
my mind and my body melts into yours
and yearns to remain there until my last breath...

That making love with you is the most real thing I felt
and that I could not imagine sharing my body
and my soul with any other man than you.
That you consume my thoughts
even when I am not thinking about you
that I miss you when you are gone
your smile
your arms
your hugs
your kiss
your voice
and I long to see you
and be with you when we are apart.

I will tell you that I am falling in love with you
and that you are breaking down my walls.
And that I will love all the parts that make you
as long as you will have me.

I want to see you at your best
and your worst
I want to know your insecurities
and your strengths
I want to share your goals
and dreams
and all that inspires you.

That I will love the crazy in you
when no one else can.
I would tell you to choose me,
because I believe in you
I see the beauty in you;
I appreciate your kindness and gentleness
and will learn to live with your weaknesses
but love your strengths.
And support you even when you are restless
and unsure.

I will Love your quirkiness
passion and drive
I will stand by your side
through all that life throws at us.

I will remind you to smile
and feel secure even in the quiet moments
when silence falls between us.

So fall in love with my sometimes impatient moods
my jealous mind
or that I sometimes feel nothing at all.

That I love too hard or too much
fall in love with the things that make me far less than perfect
my body how it widens by my hips
and bum
how I sometimes feel insecure or criticise myself.
My scars
        and marks
                and my imperfections.
I may be unconventional
with an untamed heart but I'll be true to my words
to myself and to you.

Loveless games

Aaahhh these loveless games we humans play...
One minute you're hot and in seconds you're cold.
I bear the scars of words you told...
Emotions run high and then they run dry
the untold secrets they unfold
and your words to me no longer hold.

Let's stop this madness before we grow old
let's stop wasting time if you are mine...
Or set me free and let me be me.

For I seek only a pure and selfless love.

More

More...

He makes me feel excited; he makes me feel alive, passionate, calm happy, loved, fearless and wanted...

Possibly the best thing we can do for the ones we love is to make them feel *more*...

...*More* worthy, accepted, wanted and needed.
Always so much *more* than what they would expect.

More Love...

Heart beat

My heart beats for you a thousand miles
and with just one look and your warming smile
my heart skips a beat and all the while time stands still...

As I catch my breath
this pounding beneath my chest
I know in that moment my heart would be forever yours.

But for love

My heart is breaking
My soul is aching
The loss is too much to bear.

When you love someone so much with all you have to give
you are no longer just one person;
you are two people who have become one.

You share everything your joy
your sadness your fears
your darkest secrets
laughter
pain
trust
and memories.
You fight you make up
you kiss you make love
you thank god every day for bringing this person into your life
and you do this knowing it won't last forever.

Because people die
people change
people fall in and out of love.
You give away so much of yourself
but in end that person leaves and they take a part of you away with them…

But for love you would do it all over again.

Never changing

It is a silent movement flowing through my mind
devouring my thoughts

Darkness into light.

Capturing all emotion is unlikely;
we are all substances of our own Divine.

Always changing
always wanting
forever seeking and never satisfied...

Yet never changing.

Once in a lifetime

Once in a lifetime you think you meet "the one"
The one you sat up with for hours
talking about everything and nothing
your dreams
your goals
your desires
your fears
your life past and present.
Your connection becomes so deep and strong
you cannot imagine being with anyone else.

You talk about building a life together
your perfect wedding
having children
a house with a garden
maybe even a horse.
You cried and laughed
you joked and played
you shared everything sacred and secret to your own heart
good and bad or sad.
You opened up and let go of your fear
fear of falling
fear of trusting
fear of being hurt
you let down your walls...
And you let him in completely
accepting your differences
and embracing the new.

You went on adventures
you took long walks holding hands
you made time for each other
you cooked meals together
shared deserts
drank wine
dancing while sharing your favourite songs
watching movies till you fell asleep...

Cuddling through the night
kissing till your last breath...
Making love and loving each other fiercely.
Sharing precious moments and creating new ones...
Then as the days and weeks and months go by you start to drift
you start to think that perhaps
what you had is now a distant memory
and as the cracks appear
suddenly it's annoying to be sad or unhappy
suddenly the words you speak become echoes in your own ear
your voice becomes smaller and your thoughts become your own...

...Suddenly you are lonely even though you are not alone...

Brave

One of the bravest things we can do is love someone else
completely without judgment.

One of saddest things we will learn is that sometimes
we are not enough.

And one of the biggest lessons we will learn
is no matter how much we fight to hold on
letting go is the only way for us to move forward.

Desert of my dreams

In the desert of my dreams

I awake in the quiet noise under the full moon.

Unseen in the dark I look around

and wonder where you are.

I seek to catch the wind as a thousand thorns entwine my heart.

I suffer in this silence

the earth

and the tears that flood this drought...

Heartache

This heartache...
It comes on in waves
one minute you think you are over him
you are happy and you believe you have finally moved on
and let go
and the next you are floored
tears streaming down your face as the memories flood your mind
of the love you once shared.
You read old messages and look at photos
and wonder how it went so wrong...
You question yourself
analysing each chapter of your past searching for answers
clues
and tell-tale signs
yet you reach the same empty page
So you have to close the book and remind yourself
that the love you shared were segments of joy
of what could have been, of a story which had to be told.
A lesson
a gift
and a start to something new
something you will forever hold onto.
And as the days and months and years pass by
you will be reminded that the best story of your life
is yet to unfold.

My life

This is life

upside down

unpredictable

somewhat questionable and intense

but filled with passion

love

drive

and a deeper sense of belonging.

This life I chose to live

This life that has thrown me every angle of hurt

betrayal

anger

love

meaning

questioning

longing

wanting

craving

needing

happiness and fulfilment.

But never regret.

I regret not who I was

who I am

and who I have become.

I regret not who I made

and brought into this world
for they were made out of love
and not Shame.

I do not regret the love I chose to give
and the love I chose to take away
The friendships I made
and the friendships I lost...
Because this is my life
and no one else's to live.

A world forever changing

In world forever changing I want to be the one to make you laugh
have deep conversations with, drink coffee with
go for long walks holding hands
kiss and make love with.
In a world forever changing
loving someone and being loved in return is the greatest
most unselfish gift you can share.
In a world forever changing
I want to be your partner
your lover
your friend
your future.

My demise

The watchful gaze your eyes lay upon mine in search of what?

Dare I ask?

As you put your hand in mine
I let you.

Even after all the disappointments
I forgive you.

I drown in our kiss
of the longing I've missed.
Tighter you hold onto me as the night goes by

Could this be it?

Do we give it another try?
Your sweet smile and the passion in your eyes...

Is this the new beginning of our lives?
Or is this just my demise?

Seekers

We are seekers

We are all seeking for something

            Someone to fill the spaces

the gabs...

      ...and the time.

Weekend lover

Here we are again...
The same place the same time
again and again like Groundhog Day.
You say let's take it slow and see where this goes...
So each time I give you a piece of me
knowing you have all of me...
You want to be my lover
but not my significant other
so where do we go from here
where do we draw the line?
When your kiss is like chocolate and your mouth is like wine...

Again

I hope you fall in love again
because without love our souls are empty.

This is me

This is me and I come naturally
I am not a cover on a magazine that the world perceives me to be.
I am curves and I am lines
I am truth behind these eyes of the years I have lived
and all the tears I have cried.
I am long summer days and endless nights;
I am a mother
a friend
a lover
a trend.
I am peace
I am joy
I am laughter
I am love.
I am heart breaks and heart aches
that I've shared through the years.
But I am enough.
I am a journey of ups
and I've travelled the downs but I've stayed true to myself
even in moments of doubt.

So fuck society and all that it claims be.

Be who you are
and not what others want you to be.

Life

Another day gone from this crazy life we call living.

What if

What if I kissed you stealing the breath from your mouth would you love me and never a moment doubt.

Original

Why be what everyone else wants you to be?

When you can be you.

Be original.

Liquid

*Our lives are like liquid
we flow into e*
        a
        c
        h

        o
        t
        h
        e
        r

Playlist

When I gave you my heart I gave you all of me...

Every beat of my rhythm

my melody

my song

so take me and play my strings to the beat of your drum...

Let's make music

and make me your play list till the break of dawn.

Music

When music moves you to tears
and reaches into your soul
the deepest most gratifying sense comes over you.
Relish in that moment and soak it in.
Explore the million pieces of joy
love
    anger
        happiness
            sadness
                comfort
satisfaction
content bursts of excitement within you.
Feel it
    hear it
        and *express it*

That is **now**
That is **you.**

That is...
Music

Find your way back

When someone breaks your heart
they break it in such a way
that you have shattered pieces streaming out your chest;
It seeps through your pores
and delivers the pieces of what once was your heart
to your feet on the floor.
With that it breaks your trust
your feelings of security
and the memories you held onto so tightly
For the fear of letting go was to let go
of what you felt
of what you had
letting go of yourself.
Only when you are so low that you feel you can no longer go on
after the sadness
the anger
the grief
and the pain you find your way back.

No quick fix

Sometimes
           you can't fix
                      everything;
sometimes
           you just have to let the
broken
                stay *broken*.

Another life

We are worlds away and centuries apart
yet you come to me in my dreams.
You have the face of so many

Who are you?

Forever changing
forever calling
forever waiting.
I am here come to me
embrace me
explore me
love me
want me
and take me

I am yours.

Undone

Without you I am empty...

Without you the pieces of my heart don't fit...

Without you my world seems small...

Come to me
and let me love you

Come to me
we are better as one

Come to me
and let's kiss under the sun and beneath the stars

Let the oceans move the tides
and moon swallow the shadows that hide in the dark...

Come to me
with your warm touch and the fire in your eyes

Come to me
once more and let's give in to the night.

Love that came without warning

You are the love that came without warning
you were the one to break down my walls
you had you my heart
my body
my soul

and I believed you when you said you would stay.

But you were the love that left without warning.

You are the one that broke me
and I am the one that loved you this *way*.

But you left me anyway

Then why did you leave?

You say you never loved anyone the way you loved me.
But you left me anyway.
You say with me
the world stands still when we are together.
But you left me anyway.
You say you asked the universe
to send you someone good in your life
and you found me.
But you left me anyway.
You say you want to share your life with me
build a house and have some kids.
But you left me anyway.
You say one day we will get married
and that I am your happy place.
But you left me anyway.
You say that I am the best thing that's ever happened to you.
But you left me anyway.
We loved deeply
pure and raw.
But you left me anyway.
You say you cannot imagine your life without me.
But you left me anyway.
You say I deserve everything in the world.
But you left me anyway.
You say that I am beautiful
passionate

sweet and wonderful.
But you left me anyway.
You say you are the happiest you have ever been.
But you left me anyway.
You cried with me when times were difficult
and laughed with me when times were good.
But you left me anyway.
We fought and made up
we kissed and made love.
But you left me anyway.

There is so much more you said
so much more we promised to each other
but now this all seems insignificant.
Because you left anyway.

You don't see me

You see what you only want to see...
You mock you joke
you call me sad
unrealistic and crazy...

But who are you?

You do not know what is under this skin
this skin that is me
my soul
my breath
my heart beat
the passion burning within me
my love
drive and desire...

A desire to break out and be free
a need to be wanted and accepted
A love to feel without fear or questioning my ulterior motives
My heart beating through every inch of my flesh
and each day that brings sadness and joy.

A reality...

Reality of belonging on this place we call earth...

Is it so hard to believe that beneath all this skin
I may actually be real?

Invisible strings

Invisible strings hold us together

Even in the distance

I know you will search the end of the earth to find me

For my heart only knows yours

until you are once again beside me.

Love

Love the heart that *hurts* you.

Don't hurt the heart that *loves* you.

Stepping stones

What you see is what you get.
I may not be the dream girl you long for if you are still searching.
I may not be the one you book a trip within short notice to get away.
I may not be the one you can grab a spontaneous night out with
                                                                at a whim.
I may not be the one you make love to all hours through the night
                    while we drink coffee in bed and sleep in late.
I may not be the one who makes your heart skip a thousand beats
                                when you look at into my eyes.
I may not be the finer choice of words when I express myself.
I may not always be the lively person
                                you once knew all those years ago.
I may not always be positive and happy.
I may not be the gung-ho
yoga fanatic
healthy eating vegetarian you would probably prefer.

I may not be a lot of things...

                    But what I am is genuine.

I am imperfect but I am real.
I am laughter, yells and tears.
I am sometimes up and sometimes down.
I am conversation during a home cooked meal.
A shoulder to cry on when all seems lost.
I am the writer behind the screen.

I am a Mother
a partner
a lover
a friend and
I am faithful, honest and loyal to the end.

I am truth in my words
                         and lived many lives behind these eyes.

I am a heart full of love and a soul full of sacrifice.

I am madness and strangeness all wrapped up in one.

But I am me
unique
beautiful
courageous and **strong.**

I am not a stepping stone till something better comes along.

I am You are

I am *not* what *I think I am*
You *are* what *I think I am*

Expression

Expression of one self is beautiful.
Don't hide yourself or your feelings
for fear of rejection or being judged.
The right people will see you
and adore you for who you are.
Be you
stay real
smile
laugh
forgive
believe
let go
and *love again.*

Counter tops

It's these counter tops you ravaged me on...

Naked and bare you pulled my hips to yours
kissing me with such deep desperation
ripping the layers from my body
hands searching
grabbing and finally entwining
holding on tightly.

An aching need consuming us.
You loved me forcefully
you loved me raw
you loved me painfully
yet tenderly and I was yours.

Forgiveness

If tomorrow never comes
I will know that I was loved unconditionally
and passionately by one of the most incredible people in my life.

I will know that even in the face of fear and sadness
I had a best friend
partner and lover
and of all the mistakes I made in my life
you were the biggest regret of all.

For I loved you more than I loved myself
yet I hurt you more than anyone else.
And I will forever be deeply sorry for losing you.
But I have to learn to forgive myself and let go
and move on.

Fleeting moment

A fleeting moment is all it took for her heart to fall
and soak up the lies that sounded so good.

In the still of the darkness
where she stood mesmerized by his beauty
the taste of his kiss upon her lips
the lust that fell from his mouth into hers.

She longed to believe
believe that this was it
that she was still capable of love
and being loved...

What is love?

What is love if it's not worth fighting for?
But what is worth fighting for if it's not love?
It gets harder not to stop
Loving someone even if you have been left
in the most unthinkable way.

You are worthy

The world is at your feet
what are you waiting for?
Time is now or never.

So say what's on your mind
be courageous
be silly
be uncomfortable
be emotional
and be **bold.**

Laugh
love
touch
cry
scream
feel emotion
feel scared but fear nothing.

Be you
be unique
be deep
be happy
but most of all be fierce.

Forget the hurt
move on
regret nothing.

Love life and everything it has to offer.
Love yourself!

Take time away to clear all the cobwebs from your mind
and embrace the woman you have become
the woman *you* are.

So here is to **strong** woman all around the world.

You are beautiful
passionate
amazing
and deserve all the happiness
love
laughter
and blessings the universe has to offer.

Never doubt yourself
not even for one moment.
Never settle for less.
And remember you are worthy of so much more!

Your spell

The day I fell for you
my heart pounded beneath my chest
so loud I swear the whole world could hear.

My stomach felt weak
my body shivered under your touch
and when we kissed
I knew things would never be the same.

The sky clear above us
the ocean wide before us
I got lost in your kiss
while the world around us
stood still.

This beautiful stranger
I am on the edge of danger
how could I not see you cast your spell on me!

Surrendered kiss

When you decide to kiss for the first time
that kiss is the most pivotal.

It determines everything
about where the relationship will go.

It is stronger than the final surrender
because within the kiss
you have already succumbed

to

the

surrender.

When is it my turn?

When will my forever after come into my life?
When will someone wake up next to me
look at me and see forever.

When will I be enough

When will I be the one

When will I be the face you want to see every morning
and every night when we wake and go to sleep
When will my body
my lips
my skin
my mind
be all you'll ever need.

When will my mouth be the only one you want to taste
When will my voice be the only one you want to hear
When will I be the only one you want to love
over and over
until your dying day
When is it my turn?

The forest

In the forest they descent on a lazy Saturday afternoon
hand in hand they walk under the pale blue sky.

Lush green surrounds them
glances exchange
and they both smile.

They lay down on the soft grass the earth has to offer
embraced in each other's arms they hold each other tightly
telling stories in the clouds of how two lovers met...

Facing each other they begin to kiss
softly with trembling hands
they caress each other gently.

Heat radiates between them
as their kiss grows deeper
breaths escape their mouths
as their passion grows stronger.

A slow motion of love unfolds between them
and all they can do now is surrender.

Two hearts

Two sacred hearts drowning in love.

One is open
and one is guarded.

Like poker
they remain unreadable.

But they both gamble
in the game called love.

My favourite painting

Colours *shimmer* before me
Red
yellow
blue
and green.
Figures silhouetted in the distance

Rain falls upon me.

I dance in delight at your sight
there you are your beauty unseen
under the crescent light
where *we* meet once more.

Ultimate sacrifice

If I gave you the ultimate sacrifice
how would *treat* my heart?

Would you love it quietly only for yourself to see
or would you *love it loud* and *scream it to the world.*

Lovers

Two souls
Two lovers
Two heartbeats

One love.

A promise

The moment you say I do.
An everlasting promise to give yourself
over to one another wholeheartedly.

A promise to love one another eternally.

A promise to be faithful to each other
not just in body but in mind too.

Day by day
week by week
month by month
and year by year.

A promise to hold your love so deep
and your truth so dear.
A promise to accept each other
through and through
to love without boundaries
to encourage
to support
to nurture
to care.

A promise to stand by one another no matter what life
and the future may put in your path.

A promise to be the best part of each other
in sickness and health
through laughter and tears
in all the times shared
throughout the years
till death do you part.

Un-kissed

All over

every inch

no patch of skin will go *un-kissed*

In the sun

in the rain

say it to me again

and again...

I am so in awe of the man that I adore.

Poetry and dreams

The darkness brings with a sensational quiet
you are near as nearer as heaven can be.

Naked as freedom blooms
with a cold beer in the heated night
made of poetry...
              ...and dreams

Love child

A tiny seed you grew within me
I dreamt about you before we created you
your face soft and smooth
your mouth turned up into the biggest smile
your wavy brown hair
and your bright green eyes looking back at me
you were two maybe three
and in my waking hour I knew one day
I would meet you.

That day has come
and all the fibres in my body knows
it's you
just a tiny speck you will develop
and grow into an incredible little human
even on my worst days riddled with sickness
nausea and headaches the comfort of knowing
I will be able to hold you in my arms in just a few months
is a reward no one can take away.

But I have been disillusioned...

Darkness fills the cracks in my broken heart
the pain is so unbearable
I long to drown in the pool of my blood.
Tears stream down my face as the sadness grips
and engulf my entire being...

I want to open my mouth and scream...

Help

I cannot breathe.

Your small fragile body
I will never feel in my arms
your beautiful face
I will never see
I will not hold your tiny hands in mine
and smell the scent of your delicate skin.
You will never know the love I have for you
in my heart
and soul
or the kisses
I would put upon your cheeks.

You will never see the love
and happiness in my eyes while I looked down at you
or feel the steady beat of my heart
and the quiet comfort of a mother's love
while we form a bond
no one would ever break.

We will never hear the sound of your laughter
or the joy you bring into our lives
we would never see you grow

or hear the pitter-patter of your little feet
running through the house
we will never tuck you into bed
or read you stories
and kiss you good night.
I will never meet that face I saw in my dream...

You will never meet your family that waits.

I pray in Heaven you will remain among the angels
you will grow wings and be loved without any doubt.

Your soul free and alive.

The spaces between us

I felt the essence of you flowing through me
you captivated my soul and I let you in.
I lost myself in-between the spaces between us.

You moved me like liquid drenched in your love
and I longed to stay wondering in your dark
and mysterious world.

But I had to let you go
you were always in search of something more.

But on you I have left my mark
pieces of me and what once was my whole heart
and someday you will look back to that first moment we met
that first glance
the first smile
our first words
that first touch
our first kiss.

You will be reminded of the happiness
and of the secrets
and love we shared
but one day that memory will fade
like the pages from a sun kissed book
and in time you will wonder if that was really us...

All that will be left are the *spaces* between us.

Letting go

Through all the pain and hurt and loss
I was too blind to see what lay before me.
I was so wrapped up in my own pain and sorrow
I could not see further than today
and lost out on tomorrow.

I did not see love before me
I could not understand why you hurt me so?
...and then let me go.

Only as time passes by we start to question why.
And I guess that is something I will never know.

Dance with me

Dance with me under the moonlight
Dance with me in summer sun
let's feel the earth beneath our feet
and dance to rhythm of our heart beats.
Dance with me under the galaxy of stars
and let us embrace the music of our lives.

Thank you

Thank you for everything
you gave to me during our time together
Thank you for trying to be a better man
Thank you for the laughters
Thank you for making me smile
Thank you for wiping my tears in times of sadness
Thank you for the hugs
Thank you for the kisses
Thank you for holding my hand

Thank you for telling me I am beautiful
Thank you for spoiling me in your own way
Thank you for caring for me
Thank you for teaching me new things
Thank you for all the adventures together
Thank you for your time
Thank you for being kind
Thank you for your understanding
Thank you for your support
Thank you for my morning cuddles

Thank you for my morning coffee
Thank you for taking time out of your day,
to call me and check in on me
Thank you for your love
Thank you for being there for me when I lost myself
Thank you for reminding me to eat
Thank you for reminding me to love myself

Thank you for the hurt
Thank you for the pain
Thank you for teaching me a valuable lesson

Thank you for setting me free.

Reminiscing

Time is fluid...

Days
months
years
go by and suddenly we are back in each other's lives.
Talking
reminiscing of a faded past
but the memories still fresh in our minds
and imprints of you still on my heart.
Your voice a beam of light
and a comfort to my soul
the laughter you bestow upon me
the conversations flow.
And yet the thought of why
how
where
and when still remains unknown.
But stories we shall tell and share
we will fill the blank pages with our thoughts
laughter
and words.
And within the open spaces
                        ...they will fill the air.

Life happens

And sometimes life happens...

...You stumble you fall and you hit your face against the floor
you get up and you carry on because this is not the end
you are not done.

And then life happens...

Opportunities open doors you never dreamt of
and when that door opens you run through it
and catch every dream you ever chased
because this may be the life you have been destined for...

...This is the beginning.

Conversations

Like rolling waves you hypnotise me
even throughout the distance you mesmerize me.

Your words are spoken with passion and fire
and relieves within me a knowing desire.

Your mind is filled with colour and soul
fill me up until I'm whole.

Speak to me
        sing to me
                read to me
                        while our story unfolds.

For this is now
and tomorrow is then
but today I share with you my friend.

Destiny

I stand and watch and listen and think.
You're in my mind imprinted like ink.

I linger

I touch

I breathe

I see

I am

I feel

I'm me

I am free.

I seek to know the questions unasked;
I seek to know your secrets untold.
Can this be true and is this real
is this our time
just me and you.

Is this our path, our journey through life
is this our destiny *yours* and *mine*.

...In love...

I am so in love
with the thought of being
in love with you.

Stolen

I will kiss your lips
                        stealing the breath from your mouth
and the words from your thoughts.

I will I am

I had a walk and I lay on the sand.
I looked into the heavens and asked myself
why do I not feel worthy of such a love?

The wind picked up.

They say the wind is a women's wrath...
I don't know.
What I do know is that the universe has brought us together.
Yes
I believe that too.
For whatever reason it may be
I'm willing to find out.

Name

You can say my name till the end of time
and I will never tire of hearing my name
                                          fall from your voice.

Blind love

We are like two blind people
trying to get to know each other over the phone.
We close our eyes and listen...
Listen to the breathing.

Hints of...
High
low
calm
excited
sexy
sweet
      ...Tones
And all the undertones we don't see or feel.
The magnitude of everything put together.

A much higher level.

Getting to know me

So you say you know me well

So well, too well, we have stories to tell.

So you say together we will conquer all

we will, we can, together we shall weather each and every storm.

Each tide brings something new

something sweet, something kind, something creative

something we call this crazy beautiful love.

Learning from each other

I believe in you.

Something like a phenomenon

Explosions and fireworks.
All that has been said and left unsaid
When *I speak* to you
When *I gaze* into you.

Passion and curiosity.

We will explore
Our bodies
Our minds
Our hearts.

Adventure of two lost souls
Finding each other.
Shifting.
Learning.
Being.

...Something like a phenomenon

Picture this

Bundled Clouds
Rolling over each other.
Picture perfect moments
Sitting here.

Just.

Seeing the clouds.
Blue skies a playground
for birds and seagulls alike.

Holy Shit.
The sun is hot
I kid you not.
The sun is *really* hot

A swim later?

Let's walk the earth together

Warrior and angel of light
we walk the earth together
and together we shine so bright
together we fight the fight
and embrace the truth
and accept the pain
and make it our *own*.

We sacrifice our hearts for others hurts
and wait our turn
our turn for truth
for strength
for life
for love...

...*Together* our light shines through world and earth.

Tides

The tide comes in and goes out
yet the waves always surrender to the moon.

Beautifully poetic.

Speak to me

Warrior of light
you speak to me in ways only you and I can understand.
You show me magic of another time.
We build portals to dream
and share
and dance
and sing.

You take my fears and I let you in.
You caress my tender soul with your words.
You undress my layers of hurt with your heart.
You touch my spirit with your joy.
You kiss my mind with your thoughts
and infect me with your love.

A kiss so fair

The moon is enticing
The waves hypnotic.
The pebbles are hard

I sit and stare.

The air
salty on the breeze
Fresh like a kiss so fair.

Hypnotic.

Thinking of you

Colour and fun.
Endurance and Patience.
Stamina and Creativity.
Brilliance all round with a Kiss in each drop
each splash of paint.

Waves of Love
Bears
Pythons and Hugs

Throughout the day...
We guide with Courage and Strength.
Thinking of you.

Love juice

Fumbling craziness of the unknown
two souls
two minds
two hearts
two lovers
one love.

Touching
feeling
tasting
licking
breathing
skin on skin
electric currents radiating the heat that flows within...
...letting go...
so much bliss
mouth to mouth
lips on lips
tongues entwined sealed with our kiss.
Bottled love juice.

Let's have fun tonight

Cascading clouds with melodies and rhythm
of a welcoming thunder storm
our spirits entwined...

Let's have fun tonight.

We bounce off the fluffy clouds
And fill our lungs with laughter!
Childlike happiness.

That's what we would like...

Wrap each other up in our warmth and hugs.
We will harness the lightening
to replenish our strength and energy.
We will use the thunder
to build up our courage and determination.
We will use the moon to express the love within us...
...And help us shine brightly so we don't get lost in the dark.

Let's have fun tonight.

We will meet at the Bridge of Destiny
a bridge with no end or beginning
it's just there.
Made of golden light a glow that filters into the night...
A forest awaits us, only for us.
A kaleidoscope of colours

always moving
flowing into each other with flowers entwined
in its struts and beams.

Wispy kisses guide us to a passionate embrace...
Tonight we have fun in the clouds
the forest and the galaxies
For all the heavens to see!

The bridge of...

I feel the echo beneath my feet
wind
 sand
  storm
  stone
earth and sea.
My heart becomes a raging beat
listen to the undertones let the vibrations caress your soul.

You flow through me
                with me
                        beside me.
You make love to my mind with your words.

You paint my heart with gold
with you I abandon all thought
with you I want to grow old.

I jump
       I leap
              I bound into the abyss
meet me on the bridge of destiny
Where adventure awaits us.

Thoughts and shared words

The truth is us
You + Me = *We*
You + I = *Us*

Comfortable silence
Crickets
Melodic sound
Fisherman on the beach
Sacred.
scared...
...Place of Love

Rare.

Tantric bliss

A kiss tingles.
A hug comforts.
Tantric sensations
Harmonious vibrations.
Thoughts Immense
Intense.

Full body release
absorbing
melting
being...

...It all turns into an amalgamation of Trantric bliss.

Song

The world is our song
made of shadows and light
kaleidoscopes of colours
water and earth all wrapped into one.
Waiting for us to dance in its core.

Adventure

In the Forest we will venture

In the caves we will find

In the treehouse we will love

In the clouds we will fly

In our arms we will lie.

Dance floor

Kiss me
sway me to the beat of the music
until our mouths touch
your breath warm
and sweet against my lips my pulse quickens as you wrap
your arms around me and suddenly we are alone
alone in this chaos
alone on this earth
the noise becomes silent, and then there is none.

A kiss so blissful my world stands still
Our kiss grew deeper and my heart grew louder
every fibre in my body came alive
and I felt like all my dreams came true in just one night.

I let go.
I fall...
    ...Into the deep abyss of your exquisiteness.

I let go.

I fall into you.

I see you

Let me see you with my eyes
let me strip you bare.
I want to look
I want to see
I want to touch
I want to stare.

Let's sit quietly in the comfort of our silence
Let's explore
Let me into your soul and into your mind.

Past, present and future through another dimension and time.
Together we will evoke emotions we never thought we'd known
together we will see things
hear things
feel things and make it our own.
Exquisite in this silence in the unknown.
I see you.

Verbal abuse

You beat upon me with your words
You yell
you scream.

It hurts
It *hurts*.

I shy away from your angered face
Trapped in my thoughts of this forsaken place
So vile the words pour from your mouth
Help I am drowning in my doubt.
I close my I eyes and say aloud is this me?
                                        Am I real?
                          Is this how love is meant to feel?

I swallow my thoughts and bury your words
for no longer will I allow them to hurt.

No longer am I insecure.

I seek truth in words of love that's pure
No longer do your words hold
I let them wash over me *black to gold.*
No longer am I insecure

I know now what I am worth.

Shadows and gold

It's like the first time we met,
and started talking on the phone.
      Excitement mixed with subtle shyness
          mixed with me wanting to yell out to the world
               that I am talking to the man of my dreams.

A man made of
      shadows and gold.

A man that has captured my soul.
I want to get lost in you
and you in me
and together we will drown in our love.

Tender words

We make love to each other's soul
We kiss our hearts with our mouths
You taste my lips
I taste yours.

Above and below...

...Tender words will soon be tender kisses.

Lucky love

Lucky Love
Let me hold your hand
Feel my love
It's unique.

You + I = Us

Waking dream

A kiss upon your lips so fair
I wake to dream
but you're not there...

Car crash

In an instant it happens
Words said between us
I say we need a break
you say our love is enough
I say maybe not...

Rain pours upon the roof of our car
Driving in the dark
My mind turns the matters of my heart
You look at me and say
listen...
...You are all I need
And then it happens

   CRASH

Metal smashed
Glass shatters
Car crashes and crashed lives
My life flashes before my eyes
Thrown in the depths of despair
Memories come flooding in
Not a moment to spare.

I Love You.

   CRASH

Can we go back to where we began?

Me

I am...

Bold
brave
strong.
Happy
silly
original.

Free.

I am me.

Log out...

Everyone is so hooked on connection
yet they *forget* how to be
                        c o n n e c t e d.

"A happy cry is...
...a beautiful ending"

*Written by my
beautiful daughter, April.*

Printed in Great Britain
by Amazon